Storm Warnings

By Don Basham
Introduction and personal application
by Bob Mumford

LIFECHANGERS ®

P.O. Box 3709 ❖ Cookeville, TN 38502
931.520.3730 ❖ lc@lifechangers.org

PLUMBLINE

Published by:

LIFECHANGERS ®
LIBRARY SERIES

P.O. Box 3709 | Cookeville, TN 38502
(800) 521-5676 | www.lifechangers.org

All Rights Reserved
ISBN 978-1-940054-15-5

Introduction

By Bob Mumford

The years have proven the sheer personal privilege to have heard Don Basham personally teach this very message in 1976. Its truth became a part of my "spiritual pantry," meaning I have returned to these principles repeatedly to do the very thing Don was teaching us. This is Don Basham's opportunity to speak to us again lessons that are most valuable. If you would, attempt to consider this Plumbline as Don's gift to you. It will reward you greatly!

While I was in the midst of a present storm, an unusual thing happened: as a Father, God began to deal with me about having displayed an attitude. All of you know that I am simply far too spiritual to have any sort of attitude, especially an essentially negative attitude that references back to God.

Attitude, if we tried to define it, seems to reduce to a form of measurement that reveals how totally stubborn and intensely committed we are when it comes to having our own way! "All we like sheep have gone astray each to his/her own way" (Isa. 53:6). This may summarize the sheer essence of spiritual failure and serve as the primary reason for all three kinds of storms Don presents.

While in Wal-Mart, I watched with both chagrin and wonder while a young mother lost the storm surrounding her ability to correct her 3-year-old son. He instinctively (from the original fall of man) had learned a tremendously effective way of getting his own way! It is called *Rubber Legs*. In defiance, he simply went limp. He appeared to lose all strength in both of his legs and fell to the floor. The mother was paralyzed, unable to do anything with him. Embarrassed, she pleaded with him, which increased his display and fits of temper. He was triumphant when she gave him the toy that he demanded. A seeming miracle followed. Suddenly, strength returned to his legs, and they both walked off! The mother lost. The child won. I was humbled to shame and tears. I could see the Kingdom in living color! A Father who loves us was taking the time and effort to make things increasingly clear.

As Father, God was seeking to give me an attitude demonstration. As I watched, the Lord began to speak. How grateful I am that His voice was not on the speaker system in the store!

Here is what He said: "Hebrews 12:11–13." I could hear this speaking as if it were coming from an ear-piece in my very own ear:

> *All discipline for the moment seems not to be joyful, but sorrowful; yet to those who have been trained by it, <u>afterwards it yields the peaceful fruit of righteousness.</u> Therefore, strengthen the hands that are weak and the knees that are feeble,* (rubber legs) *and <u>make straight paths for your feet, so that the limb which is lame may not be put out of joint,</u> but rather be healed (Heb. 12:11-13).*

I saw it immediately: He really cares about our healing.

Storms of life are all various forms of testing. When I do not want to be tested, I learn how to avoid what Father is asking. How? Do the Rubber Legs Syndrome. I am too weak, too dumb, too innocent. I pretend not to know what is happening, so I can go limp. I will do anything but respond with maturity!

We all, none excluded, seek to avoid "taking exams." It is a form of evaluation. We are petrified of being evaluated. We are never good enough, smart enough, or able to take the exam. Remember the amount of anxiety when we took our first driver's exam? Calling in sick on the day of an exam for which we are unprepared is common enough in the academic world. It is Rubber Legs Syndrome!

Note in Don Basham's instruction that in only one of the storms are we asked to hide. The other two are designed to produce human responsibility and evaluate where we are in truth. God seeks to reveal in us "little faith" as contrasted to where we are in our own exaggerated thinking. Remember, Grace is more than unmerited favor: "He gives Grace to the humble" and "resists the proud" (Jas. 4:6). Both of these are attitudes!

We are now getting ready to read or re-read Don's instruction. Each storm, both the mini and the mega, is Father's gift. He is in them all. He is in the ones you do not like and the ones of which you are afraid. We can all go rubber legs! We collapse and intentionally do all we can to prove "No one can make me walk!" We gather the sympathy and get our own way. When the next life-storm comes, we are unable to embrace the storm because we are now totally unprepared. *Yes, Father does care about your deeper and urgent healing!*

False faith is revealed in the storm. Inadequate faith is revealed in the storm. True faith can now be seen in human action. Endurance is taking hold. Boldness is becoming real. Each storm has its own lesson. We need all three in order to move from spiritual infancy into Rhema forms and expressions of maturity (Heb. 5:12-14).

Storm Warnings

By Don Basham

Confirming the souls of the disciples, and exhorting them to continue in the faith, and that we must through much tribulation enter into the Kingdom of God (Acts 14:22).

Years ago when I was in seminary in Oklahoma, my wife and I took a brief summer vacation in Colorado. The day of the long drive home, we left quite early from our motel in Lake City, Colorado, and shortly found ourselves at the top of a 14,000 ft. mountain pass in the middle of a blinding snowstorm. Once we cleared the pass, the snow stopped and the sun broke forth. But less than an hour later, we plunged into more bad weather with cold sleet rattling down upon us.

Again the skies cleared. Then near Raton, New Mexico, we encountered still another storm. This time, hail the size of large marbles bounced on the hood and smacked the windshield so fiercely we feared the glass would break. Fortunately, that onslaught likewise proved of brief duration; and as we headed eastward across the plains of Oklahoma, we thought the time of storms was safely behind us.

But we were wrong. For in the remaining hours of our trip, we encountered a violent wind storm, followed by a dust storm that blackened the afternoon skies. We outdistanced those freakish conditions only to plunge into a rain storm so fierce that water briefly covered the highway to a depth of three to four inches. Much to our relief, we arrived home near midnight and unloaded the car under peaceful, starry skies that left no hint of the vicious storms we had encountered during that long day.

In our memories, that day in early September of 1955 is labeled as "the day of the storms." Snow, sleet, hail, wind, dust, and rain—six storms in one day. We have never experienced another day like it.

Such an experience is convincing proof that storms are part of life, and just as this is true in the natural realm, so it is in the spiritual. Spiritual storms are part of every Christian's life. It is the firm conviction of many that a day of unprecedented spiritual storms is upon us. The spiritual warfare raging in and around us continues to intensify. Both the dealings of God and the harassment of Satan are becoming more pronounced.

In this article, we will examine the various kinds of storms that break in on us and offer some advice for dealing with them.

First of all, let's define the term "spiritual storm." By that I mean those conditions, situations, and experiences that we know to be abnormal or out of balance and which place us under such physical, emotional, and spiritual pressure that we find it difficult to function normally.

The spiritual storms we encounter seem to fall

into three major categories, and our awareness of these distinct categories is essential. If we fail to distinguish the kind of storm we are in, we may have great difficulty for each of the three kinds of storms calls for a different response. First, there are storms to be rebuked or resisted. Secondly, there are storms to seek shelter from. Thirdly, there are storms to endure. Depending on the nature of the storm, there is a time to fight, a time to hide, and a time to stand.

Before we give scriptural examples of the various kinds of storms, we need to make this important point: Every storm which sweeps into our lives is allowed by God. No matter the source--be it Satan, circumstances, or the dealings of God--all storms are allowed by God and are ultimately used to serve His purposes.

STORMS TO BE REBUKED OR RESISTED

From the ministry of Jesus, we find some examples of storms that were rebuked or resisted:

Now it happened, on a certain day, that He got into a boat with His disciples. And He said to them, "Let us cross over to the other side of the lake." And they launched out. But as they sailed He fell asleep. And a windstorm came down on the lake, and they were filling with water, and were in jeopardy. And they came to Him and awoke Him, saying, "Master, Master, we are perishing!"

Then He arose and rebuked the wind and the raging of the water. And they ceased, and there was a calm. But He said to them, "Where is your faith?" And they were afraid, and marveled, saying to one another, "Who can this be? For He commands even the winds and water, and they obey Him!" (Lk 8:22-25).

Clearly, this storm was of satanic origin. To what extent Satan can affect the elements, none of us can estimate--but affect them he does! Jesus would never have rebuked the storm if it had been from God. He rebuked the demonic force causing the elements to rage, and the wind and the sea grew calm under the authority of His word.

What's more, Jesus chided the disciples for their fear. His comment--"Where is your faith?"--indicated they should have handled the emergency without His help. The Lord's spiritual impartation to us includes the ability to rebuke the demonic influences that rage around us.

Now, let's examine another kind of storm that raged against Jesus--His temptation in the wilderness:

Then Jesus was led up by the Spirit into the wilderness to be tempted by the devil. And when He had fasted forty days and forty nights, afterward He was hungry. Now when the tempter came to Him, he said, "If

You are the Son of God, command that these stones become bread." But He answered and said, "It is written, 'Man shall not live by bread alone, but by every word that proceeds from the mouth of God.'"

Then the devil took Him up into the holy city, set Him on the pinnacle of the temple, and said to Him, "If You are the Son of God, throw Yourself down. For it is written: 'He shall give His angels charge over you,' and 'In their hands they shall bear you up, lest you dash your foot against a stone.' Jesus said to him, "It is written again, 'You shall not tempt the Lord your God.'"

Again, the devil took Him up on an exceedingly high mountain, and showed Him all the kingdoms of the world and their glory. And he said to Him, "All these things I will give You if You will fall down and worship me." Then Jesus said to him, "Away with you, Satan! For it is written, 'You shall worship the Lord your God, and Him only you shall serve.'" Then the devil left Him, and behold, angels came and ministered to Him (Matt. 4:1-11).

The wilderness was a stormy 40-day period of intense spiritual struggle in which Jesus stood His ground, resisting each of Satan's attempts to divert Him from God's holy purpose. Yet, the storm was allowed by God Himself. Scripture clearly states that after His baptism in the Jordan, Jesus was "led by the spirit into the wilderness to be tempted of the devil" (Matt. 4:1).

The storm of temptation was from Satan, but it was the Holy Spirit who led Jesus into the path of the storm.

STORMS TO SEEK SHELTER FROM

There is a time to fight; there is a time to hide.

In Exodus, chapter 12, we read how Moses relayed God's instructions to the elders of Israel on how to shelter their families from the death angel, God's final plague upon the Egyptians.

> *Then Moses called for all the elders of Israel and said to them, "Pick out and take lambs for yourselves according to your families, and kill the Passover lamb. And you shall take a bunch of hyssop, dip it in the blood that is in the basin, and strike the lintel and the two doorposts with the blood that is in the basin. And none of you shall go out of the door of his house until morning. For the Lord will pass through to strike the Egyptians; and when He sees the blood on the lintel and on the two doorposts, the Lord will pass over the door and not allow the destroyer to come*

into your houses to strike you. And you shall observe this thing as an ordinance for you and your sons forever" (Ex. 12:21-24).

Notice that the promise of protection from that deadly storm was conditional. The Israelites would be spared only if they remained in the shelter of the house marked by the blood of the lamb.

"And none of you shall go out at the door of his house until the morning" (verse 22). Any first-born Israelite foolish enough to venture out of his house would die. Fortunately, every Israelite obeyed (see verse 28).

At times, storms of great magnitude arise that are to be left totally in God's hands. To rush out to rebuke these storms would prove futile and harmful because only God in His power can handle such situations. Rather than fighting, we are to seek shelter in God so that He may step forward to fight the battle for us.

There is a fascinating story of just such an incident in Israel's history in 2 Chronicles, chapter 20. In this account, the Ammonites and Moabites were massed against the nation of Judah, threatening to drive them from their God-given land. When King Jehoshaphat and all Judah gathered to pray and seek God's help, He provided this surprising answer:

And he said, "Listen, all you of Judah and you inhabitants of Jerusalem, and you, King Jehoshaphat! Thus says the Lord to you: 'Do

*not be afraid nor dismayed because of this
great multitude, for the battle is not yours,
but God's. You will not need to fight in this
battle'* (2 Chron. 20:15, 17).

With dramatic faith, Jehoshaphat appointed a regiment of singers to stand before his army praising God, and as they sang and praised the Lord, their enemies fell to fighting among themselves and destroyed each other. Because Judah had sought shelter in God's protection from this storm of opposition, God fought and won the battle for them.

Additional scriptural encouragement to seek shelter from certain storms is found in the words of the psalmist:

*Be merciful to me, O God, be merciful to me!
For my soul trusts in You; And in the shadow
of Your wings I will make my refuge, Until
these calamities have passed by (Ps 57:1).*

The introduction to Psalm 57 indicates it was written while David was hiding at the cave Adullam, seeking shelter from the wrath of Saul (see I Sam. 22:1). Remember, David wasn't seeking shelter out of cowardice. He could easily have killed Saul. Rather he hid "from" Saul's wrath out of respect for God's authority for Saul was a king whom God had anointed.

David's action is all the more significant when we realize he already knew he was Saul's successor. Yet in obedience to the purpose of God, he sought neither to justify himself nor to further his own cause. During that strange and stormy interval, it was right for David to hide. Some storms we must seek shelter from.

SOME STORMS WE MUST ENDURE

There is a time to fight, and a time to hide; there is also a time to stand.

The third type of storm that we wish to discuss is the storm we can neither rebuke nor seek to escape: it is the storm we must endure. It is my personal observation that in these days of intensified spiritual warfare, this kind of storm is appearing more and more frequently in the life of every Christian. Let's look at two scriptural examples of such storms, both from the life of Paul. The first is found in 2 Corinthians 12:7-10:

And lest I should be exalted above measure by the abundance of the revelations, a thorn in the flesh was given to me, a messenger of Satan to buffet me, lest I be exalted above measure. Concerning this thing I pleaded with the Lord three times that it might depart from me. And He said to me, "My grace is sufficient for you, for My strength is made perfect in weakness." Therefore most gladly I will rather boast in my infirmities, that the power of Christ may rest upon me. Therefore I take pleasure in infirmities, in reproaches, in needs, in persecutions, in

distresses, for Christ's sake. For when I am
weak, then I am strong.

Scholars are not agreed as to the exact nature of Paul's thorn. Personally, I do not believe it was a physical illness or weakness. It is my conviction that it was a savagely intense spiritual opposition to Paul's ministry. Paul calls it a "messenger of Satan" sent to "buffet" him. After accepting God's assurance that He would help him endure, Paul added that he was determined to take pleasure in the storm of opposition he describes as "infirmities, reproaches, necessities, persecution, and distress." The opposition to his ministry was both constant and intense. It represented a kind of storm that Paul could neither rebuke nor escape—he could only endure.

The second storm in Paul's ministry is graphically portrayed for us in Acts 27. We suggest you read the entire 27 chapter of Acts, the story of the misfortunes befalling Paul and his company as, under Roman guard, they unsuccessfully attempt a sea voyage to Rome.

Paul, apparently with insight concerning the impending misfortune, warns both the centurion guarding him and the captain of the ship that such a voyage would be dangerous. Nevertheless, the voyage is attempted, and the ship is overtaken by a terrible storm that persists for fourteen days and nights, driving their beleaguered craft 700 miles off course, westward across the Mediterranean.

Although the Bible is not given to dramatic language, the intensity of the storm is made graphically clear:

Now when neither sun nor stars appeared for many days, and no small tempest beat on us, all hope that we would be saved was finally given up (Acts 27:20).

This literal storm raises a number of spiritual questions about God's purpose in allowing storms that must be endured. Can't you imagine during the days and nights that the ship was mercilessly driven before the storm, Paul, Luke, and the rest of the small band of bewildered believers must have wondered why the storm persisted. Surely, they must have recalled how Jesus rebuked the storm and how "the winds and sea obeyed him." And hadn't He chided the disciples for their lack of faith?

Don't you suppose Paul, Luke, and the others tried to take authority over that storm? I'm sure they must have prayed, rebuked, reckoned, pleaded the blood of Christ, commanded, committed, relinquished, and practiced every other spiritual discipline. Yet nothing worked! No matter what they tried, the storm continued—it was "unrebukable."

At the peak of the storm's intensity, God sent an angel to Paul to assure him that not only would he survive the storm to preach in Rome but that the other 275 people aboard would also be spared. Isn't it odd, though, that God went to all the trouble of sending the angel and yet did nothing to stop the storm. How strange are God's ways! He wouldn't calm the storm, yet He sent miraculous encouragement to Paul in the midst of it. Thus, the Scripture make it clear: by God's intention, some storms must be endured.

WHAT KIND OF STORM?

About a year ago, as I sat at my desk preparing the basic outline of this message, my daughter Laura came up to me. "What are you working on, Daddy?" she asked.

"A message about storms," I replied, and then I described the three kinds: storms to be rebuked, storms to seek shelter from, and storms to endure. Laura listened carefully. "Sounds like it will make a good message, Daddy," she nodded, "but can I ask you one question? How do you know what kind of storm you are in?"

I laughed. "Honey, if I had all the answers to that question, I'd be the most popular Bible teacher around."

While complete understanding may be unattainable, there are some factors which can help us identify the storms.

First, it is a help just to know that all storms are not alike. Unfortunately, many Christians oversimplify spiritual matters, and there are some Christians who believe every storm should be rebuked. Others believe every storm should be avoided, and still others believe every storm must be endured.

The dangers of accepting such an over-simplified view are obvious. If we approach every storm as if it were to be rebuked (as some overly dogmatic "faith ministries" would recommend), then we never learn the wisdom of seeking God's protection or shelter. Neither would we learn important lessons that only endurance can teach us. Sometimes we would be right, but other times we would end up slugging it out in some battle God never intended us to fight. Or we may end up fighting the purposes of God Himself.

On the other hand, if we adopt the position that every storm is to be avoided, we may be right occasionally, but we may never learn to stand and exercise the authority we have over Satan in the name of Jesus. Other times we may end up trying to escape from the discipline of God.

But finally, if we treat all storms as if they are to be endured, we take needless punishment from the enemy in addition to never learning to assert the authority we have as Christians.

To apply the figure of speech we used earlier, there is a time to fight, a time to hide, and a time to stand. If all we can do is fight, we never learn to hide or to stand. If all we do is hide, we never learn to fight or stand. If all we do is stand, we never learn to fight or hide. Yet, fighting, hiding, and standing may each be a proper response in a given circumstance.

So, how can we know what kind of storm we are in so as to exercise the appropriate response?

WHEN TO REBUKE OR RESIST

Some storms are clearly satanic. The most obvious of these are those sudden and overpowering temptations that turn us aside from what we know to be the will of God. Satan knows where you and I are "temptable" even as he knew the same about Jesus. Notice how in the wilderness Satan tempted Jesus in terms of His unique powers and abilities. Satan never tempts me to turn stones into bread or to jump off the pinnacle of the temple. I don't have that kind of power to be perverted. But Jesus did.

Although He was well-disciplined in His spirit, He was, nevertheless, vulnerable to temptation in terms of His own unique gifts and powers, and that is right where Satan hit Him. But Jesus resisted Satan's persuasions, refusing to use His power selfishly to create food where there was none or to defy the law of gravity. (Significantly though, in God's perfect will and time, He later did both, multiplying the loaves and fishes and walking on the water.)

We are vulnerable in terms of our own particular weaknesses, and when storms of temptation rage against us, that is the time God expects us to rebuke and resist the enemy.

Like many Christians, for years I sought shelter from storms I knew were satanic. Because I didn't know how to fight (i.e., to rebuke Satan in the name of Jesus), I often tried to hide. And failing that, I tried miserably and often unsuccessfully to endure.

Through the deliverance ministry, I learned not

only the authority we have in Jesus' name to cast out demons but also our right and authority in His name to stand and rebuke the satanic attacks that come to us from the outside. This is the encouragement offered in James: "Submit yourselves therefore to God. *Resist* [literally, oppose] the devil, and he will flee from you" (Jas. 4:7).

Among the storms to be rebuked are those powerful assaults on the lusts of the flesh that include things like drugs, alcohol, nicotine, and sex. Earnest Christians succumb repeatedly to Satan's attacks in these areas not necessarily because they are bound by evil spirits (although this is often the case) but because they fail to utilize their authority in Jesus Christ to press an attack against the enemy. We are to rebuke! We are to resist! We are to fight! This is one kind of storm we know is from the enemy. It is always Satan who tempts us to indulge our carnal appetites, and the Scriptures clearly command us not to "fulfill the lusts of the flesh" (Gal. 5: 16-17).

Two other satanic storms take the form of attack on our emotions. One is fear, the cruel weapon that in Satan's hand can turn something as simple as an unexpected ring of the telephone or the delayed arrival of a loved one into an occasion for panic. Fear, which Satan can slip like a dagger into some unguarded crevice of our thought life to goad minor apprehension into an unreasoning dread that saps our strength and weakens our will. Fear, which can exaggerate anyone of a thousand minor aches and pains into a monstrous dread of fatal illness that will dog our steps in daytime and haunt our sleep at night.

The other storm is anger by which Satan inflames a simple irritation into a murderous rage or a mild disagreement into the destruction of a lifelong friendship.

Both of these satanic storms are relentlessly sweeping across society today, taking almost as great a toll on Christians as unbelievers. It is more than coincidental that Jesus, in describing the signs that would accompany the close of the age, speaks of "men's hearts failing them through fear" (Lk. 21:16) and of how "many shall betray one another and hate one another" (Matt. 24: 10).

But once we recognize the satanic nature of these storms and begin to rebuke and resist them with the authority available to us in the name of Jesus, we can experience the deep joy of putting the enemy of our souls to flight.

WHEN TO SEEK SHELTER

"For You have been a shelter for me, and a strong tower from the enemy" (Ps. 61:3).

Although some storms are to be fought or rebuked, at times we face storms that actually require nothing more than watchful waiting and trust under the shelter of the Holy Spirit. We see things take place that clearly indicate that God has fought our battle as surely as He did in the case of Jehoshaphat and Judah mentioned earlier.

We can suffer needless pain and buffeting by charging out to rebuke some storm that God intends to handle all on His own. I believe God sometimes allows storms of frightening proportions to loom large on our horizons simply to teach us how to "stand still" and trust in Him. Our place is merely to stay under cover, wait, and pray.

It is my conviction that the social and economic storms that are rocking our society today are storms Christians can be largely sheltered from. But sometimes we not only find shelter, we build it. Today, most alert Christians are aware of the Holy Spirit's emphasis on bringing members of the Body of Christ into responsible, committed relationships with one another. Without going into detail as to how such relationships develop, we see how they provide a real shelter from the rising lawlessness, immorality, and self-seeking materialism of our age.

Indeed, one does not have to be a prophet to see that the future holds exciting prospects for committed Christians to emerge as a counter culture, the embodiment of social and economic salvation, as well as spiritual, in a world falling apart.

I do not believe the storms of tribulation and judgment that God is allowing to come upon the world today are intended for the faithful Christian. Although we will be affected by them, we will not become casualties. In the rising flood of distress, we shall find safety in the ark of God. In a time of great and terrible shaking, we shall be found in the

Kingdom that cannot be shaken.

WHEN TO ENDURE

The first two kinds of storms we have described, storms to be rebuked or resisted and storms to seek shelter from, can only accomplish so much in us. They can bring us to the authority we have in Jesus' name and to the necessity of trusting God and abiding in His protection. Yet, there are essential qualities and divine goals to be achieved in us that neither of these two storms can produce. Neither of these storms is intended by God to touch us. Although they serve to shape our patterns of resistance and protection, they do no deep work within us. That painful task is reserved for the storms we must endure.

When I first became a charismatic Christian, I was so joyfully preoccupied with gifts and miracles that I mistakenly assumed that Christian maturity meant winning all the battles and experiencing nothing but a succession of triumphs. All it took was enough faith in God's power.

In later years, I have reached the point of thanking God that I didn't always win or always "have enough faith" and that some of my prayers were answered "no" instead of "yes." I have come to see that failure, disappointment, adversity, and suffering all have their place in God's purpose. Many unpleasant but essential lessons in living are learned in that third kind of storm; the storm we must endure.

It may come as a surprise to some happy

charismatics that God is more interested in producing *character* than He is in bestowing charisma. And what is the matrix out of which character is formed? Peter gives us a clue:

> *Beloved, do not think it strange concerning the fiery trial which is to try you, as though some strange thing happened to you; but rejoice to the extent that you partake of Christ's sufferings, that when His glory is revealed, you may also be glad with exceeding joy (1 Pet. 4:12-13).*

What is the nature of the fire that forges Christian character? Is it not trial, hardship, persecution, and --finally--crucifixion? When we learn to accept such adversity as an essential part of the Christian life, we have taken the first feeble steps in the direction of maturity.

We find confirmation of this principle in the life of our Lord Jesus who "learned obedience through the things which He suffered" (Heb. 5:8). In His lifetime, He rebuked Satan and his storms and continually ministered life to multitudes. Yet, He also suffered rejection, persecution, condemnation, and crucifixion--all storms He had to endure. And He warned His disciples:

> *Remember the word that I said to you, "A servant is not greater than his master." If*

they persecuted Me, they will also persecute you. If they kept My word, they will keep yours also (Jn. 15:20).

Without intending to sound like a martyr, I believe we are entering a time that will specialize in the storms we must endure. The spiritual warfare swirling around us intensifies daily. That old serpent--the devil, the "accuser of the brethren"--is fanning fires of accusation, slander, and condemnation between believers. It will likely get worse before it gets better since Jesus Himself identified the closing of the age as one where men would hate and betray one another (Matt. 24:10).

In addition to the storm of persecution, God Himself is bringing sharp pressure to bear on us, exposing all those traits, habits, attitudes, and indulgences still alive and healthy in most of us. In the past, it seemed that God ignored these "minor personality flaws" in our lives, but now He is relentlessly dealing with them and putting them to death. God is determined to bring forth a people who manifest both maturity and purity, both health and holiness.

According to my understanding of God's purpose in this hour, such storms of dealing we can neither rebuke nor escape. Both the persecution of the enemy and the chastening of God serve to purge out the dross hammering us into the proper shape for God's effectual use. Both accomplish something in us that blessings and miracles can never produce.

And you have forgotten the exhortation which speaks to you as to sons:

"My son, do not despise the chastening of the Lord, Nor be discouraged when you are rebuked by Him; For whom the Lord loves He chastens, And scourges every son whom He receives."

If you endure chastening, God deals with you as with sons; for what son is there whom a father does not chasten? But if you are without chastening, of which all have become partakers, then you are illegitimate and not sons. Furthermore, we have had human fathers who corrected us, and we paid them respect. Shall we not much more readily be in subjection to the Father of spirits and live? For they indeed for a few days chastened us as seemed best to them, but He for our profit, that we may be partakers of His holiness. Now no chastening seems to be joyful for the present, but painful; nevertheless, afterward it yields the peaceable fruit of righteousness to those who have been trained by it.

Therefore strengthen the hands which hang down, and the feeble knees, and make straight paths for your feet, so that what is lame may not be dislocated, but rather be healed (Heb. 12:5-13).

So let us not lose heart. Those storms that we must endure, much more than the storms we rebuke or the storms we seek shelter from, serve to fit us more perfectly into the high and holy purposes of God.

In conclusion, whether we find ourselves rebuking, hiding from, or enduring the storms that inevitably come into our lives, we can be encouraged by the fact that God is standing with us in every difficult circumstance that we face. Just as He sent a ministering angel to Paul in the midst of the storm, we know that in every blustery situation God stands ready to direct us, shelter us, or strengthen us. If we place our complete trust in Him, He will use each storm to mature us and conform us more fully to the ways of His Kingdom. *NEW WINE MAGAZINE,* February, 1976. Pgs. 24-29. © Copyright, Christian Growth Ministries, 1976.

Lessons learned from each of the storms: my own application of this most urgent impartation of lessons so vital to our Kingdom journey:

By Bob Mumford

1. Deeper, complex, more serious attitudes that hinder spiritual growth require more intense forms of storm. Therefore, we define mega and mini-storms. All storms are disruptive and have lessons. Some, however, are designed to plow the back 40 acres leaving nothing that is not uprooted and transformed. The question asked the weatherman concerning the hurricane coming ashore here in North Carolina: "What do you expect to see after the storm?" His answer: "A totally new landscape!"

2. More than likely, we can be in two or more storms at one time. Don introduced us to the reality, which over the years, has proven so much deeper and costly. Is it likely for us to embrace a relational storm (e.g., unexpected divorce) that proves to be so complex it creates a financial storm in its path? Is it possible for these two storms to create a third storm, a spiritual crisis, that would qualify as mega? That would precipitate three storms at once!

3. Every storm seeks to encourage, cultivate, and increase human responsibility. As Don so carefully instructs us, how and in what manner

we are encouraged to respond is something of the intended purpose of the event itself. Failure or refusal to respond properly precipitates an ugly attitude, one that is extremely expensive--identified as we become offended or scandalized. You can see it clearly in Matthew 11:6. Offense occurs when the Lord does something of which we, personally, do not like or approve. Yes, I am offended!

4. Some storms seem to cause a form of damage that seems irreparable. This signifies that the "answer" that we may be seeking, even demanding, may not come clear until eternity. Those of us who have been through other mega-storms understand; and though we find them intellectually uncomfortable, we are willing to wait!

5. The degree, intensity, and duration of a storm appear to be designed to last long enough and blow hard enough for us to see our own superficiality. Only the Lord knows when we have ceased serious seeking and are now living on religious clichés and memorized bible verses. Someone said: "If you want to know what the Lord is saying, begin to read all of the verses that you do not have underlined." False triumphalism simply cannot endure a mega-storm. Religiosity quits, becomes offended, or goes rubber legged. It cannot endure because it is shakable and not Kingdom.

6. The Rubber Legs Syndrome centers on increased weariness!--fainting!--I cannot take anymore!--Stop the world! I want to get off. These are all signs of refusal to embrace the storm, seeking to escape rather than respond. I have been shocked at how creative and impulsive I have been to discover and use these phrases as sophisticated pleas designed to persuade the Lord to stop what He is doing and listen to me: Lord, be wise and agreeable. Do it my way! God the Father seeks "A spirit of praise instead of a spirit of fainting" (Isa. 61:3).

7. There are some storms that are designed primarily to "press us into His Own Person":

> *In the same way the Spirit also helps our weakness; for we do not know how to pray as we should, but the Spirit Himself intercedes for us with groanings too deep for words; and He who searches the hearts knows what the mind of the Spirit is, because He intercedes for the saints according to the will of God. And we know that God causes all things to work together for good to those who love God, to those who are called according to His purpose (Rom. 8:26-28).*

A. Be aware that praying in other tongues is to be increasingly certain that you are praying in the will of God. Personal testimony: If I did not know how to "pray in the Holy Spirit," I question if I would be here to write these words!

B. My own Rubber Legs Syndrome may not allow me to pray what actually needs to be prayed. I have many examples in my journey.

C. Note that "praying in the Spirit" concluded with "All things working for the *purpose* of God." Now we are coming clear.

8. Some storms have only one declared purpose, which is redemptive: it is to set us free from our religious self (Lk 4:18). Out-dated religion may be the most dangerous entity in the universe. Note that ISIS is outdated religion. Dealing with our closely held and erroneous pre-suppositions may be the most complex and difficult task in the entire universe. Father has chosen that task for Himself. He seeks to accomplish it by use of "all things" working in your daily life. All things often come into your world by means of mini and mega storms.

9. If you will receive, guard, and embrace them, I will give you my own two personal "keys to the Kingdom." These two promises have been the guardian of my heart and instructor of my

responses. They may be hard to hear and difficult to embrace. If you will make an authentic attempt to do so, God the Father will bear witness to your human response, embracing you as one who seeks to please Him in "all things." They are

1 Corinthians 10:13. The context is spiritual warfare in the journey from Egypt to the Land of promises. Listen as we are instructed in the proper response to every storm--none excluded:

For no temptation (no trial regarded as enticing to sin) [no matter how it comes or where it leads] has overtaken you and laid hold on you that is not common to man [that is, no temptation or trial has come to you that is beyond human resistance and that is not adjusted and adapted, belonging to human experience, and such as man can bear]. But God is faithful [to His Word and to His compassionate nature], and He [can be trusted] not to let you be tempted and tried and assayed beyond your ability and strength of resistance and power to endure, but with the temptation He will [always] also provide the way out (the means of escape to a landing place), that you may be capable and strong and powerful to bear up under it patiently (1 Cor. 10:13, AMPC).

Hebrews 12:4. How very different this one is from rubber legs. How urgent for every present day believer in this nation and around the world, as we enter the a phase of "anti-Christian" sentiment:

You have not yet struggled and fought ago-nizingly against sin, nor have you yet resisted and withstood to the point of pouring out your [own] blood (Heb 12:4, AMPC).

A fatherly prayer. Trust me in this. My own journey --storms and all--is now right at 75 years. An elder knows what not to do. I now know what rubber legs actually cost us--more than we can imagine! Take authority over your own life and future. Not to worry! You have, maybe without knowing it, already given God the Father permission when you gave yourself to water baptism. There is nothing new here; it is simply acting on the awakened heart. We are seeking to act with intentionality toward God as a Father.

Pray the intention or purpose of these words as guidance for your own. Express the thoughts in your own words as far as is possible.

1. Father, I really do believe that you are concerned for my *healing*. Living as "me" has not been easy. I need you to save me from myself. Forgive my rubber legs. By grace, I will not respond in that manner in the future.
2. Actually, Father, I have some anxiety as to what

you may need to employ for the purpose of accomplishing that healing. Help me turn my anxiety into living faith and Agape maturity. I really do want to grow up. Agape does cast out fear.

3. Your past display of Agape in the Person of Christ allows me to trust you. Your compassionate nature is my refuge. Your proven actions are my inheritance. Release me from my own self-created prison. You have already proven your love for me.

4. I commit to you with all of the integrity and strength I have. I not only receive Christ, I yield to Your purpose in my life as expressed in Christ's commission to use all things to conform me to the Image of Christ.

5. All storms are common to man. I refuse to allow the voices of accusation saying "God has failed you!" to prevail.

6. Heal my offenses, known or unknown, toward You and others. Allow me to walk free. Keep me on the Agape Road that takes me home to you.

7. Father, above all, I seek to please you. My freedom depends upon a God-given ability to please another. You are my choice as the One I have chosen to please. Help me.

LIFECHANGERS®

P.O. Box 3709 ❖ Cookeville, TN 38502

931.520.3730 ❖ lc@lifechangers.org

www.ingramcontent.com/pod-product-compliance
Lightning Source LLC
Chambersburg PA
CBHW071800020426
42331CB00008B/2342